AF589763

LINDA STONE

Kravitz and Sons LLC
204 E Arlington Blvd. Suite B
Greenville, NC 27858

© 2025 Linda Stone. All rights reserved.
No part of this book may be reproduced, stored in a retrieval system, or transmitted by any means without the written permission of the author.

Published by Kravitz and Sons LLC.
ISBN: 979-8-89639-356-6 (sc)
ISBN: 979-8-89639-355-9 (e)

Library of Congress Control Number: 2025917286

Because of the dynamic nature of the Internet, any web addresses or links contained in this book may have changed since publication and may no longer be valid. The views expressed in this work are solely those of the author and do not necessarily reflect the views of the publisher, and the publisher hereby disclaims any responsibility for them.

LINDA STONE

DEDICATION

THIS BOOK IS DEDICATED TO ADAN AND MCKENZIE. YOU'RE MY REASON THIS NOW EXISTS, AND MY INSPIRATION TO CONTINUE DREAMING. I HOPE I INSPIRE YOU TO NEVER GIVE UP ON YOUR DREAMS, AND I CAN'T WAIT TO SEE WHERE THEY TAKE YOU! I LOVE YOU...TEDDY, BUBBLES AND CORKY DO TOO!

LINDA STONE HOPES TO BRING JOY AND ENCOURAGEMENT TO CHILDREN EVERYWHERE BY TEACHING THEM ABOUT THE IMPORTANCE OF ADOPTING SHELTER PETS, AND THE LOVING BONDS THAT EXIST BETWEEN THESE ANIMALS AND HUMANS.

TEDDY AND BUBBLES, HER REAL LIFE ADOPTED DOGS BOTH CAME FROM SHELTERS, AND HAVE BROUGHT LINDA AS MUCH LOVE AS SHE GIVES TO THEM. NOT ONLY ARE THESE DOGS GREAT COMPANIONS, BUT THEY ARE HIGHLY INTELLIGENT CREATURES SO WORTHY OF HAVING A SECOND CHANCE AT LIFE IN A LOVING HOME. SADLY, THERE ARE MANY ANIMALS WHO NEVER GET THAT CHANCE.

LINDA HAS MADE IT HER MISSION TO SHARE A PORTION OF ALL THE PROCEEDS OF HER BOOKS WITH SHELTERS. WHEN YOU PURCHASE ONE OF HER BOOKS, KNOW THAT YOU ARE PART OF THE MOVEMENT TO HELP SUSTAIN THESE ANIMALS UNTIL THEY CAN BE ADOPTED INTO LOVING HOMES.

THANK YOU FOR PARTNERING WITH ME THROUGH THE PURCHASE OF THIS BOOK. TOGETHER, WE REALLY CAN DO GREAT THINGS IN ASSISTING THE SHELTERS TO CARE FOR THESE PETS.

OTHER BOOKS BY LINDA STONE

BUBBLES' TROUBLES

HOME IS THE VERY BEST PLACE TO BE

I'M AN UNUSUAL DOG, AND MY NAME IS TEDDY.
I SIMPLY LOVE TO EAT SPAGHETTI!

IT'S LONG AND STRINGY AND OH SO GOOD!
IT TASTES THE WAY I WISH DOG FOOD WOULD.

I REALLY DO LOVE IT, BUT IT WASN'T ALWAYS THIS WAY.
READ ON, AND I'LL TELL YOU WHAT HAPPENED ONE DAY.

I USED TO BE HOMELESS. I DIDN'T BELONG. MY OWNER DUMPED ME BECAUSE I DID SOMETHING WRONG.

I NEEDED TO GO OUT AND COULDN'T WAIT ANYMORE. NOBODY WAS HOME, SO I WENT POTTY ON THE FLOOR.

I DIDN'T KNOW DIGGING HOLES IN THE YARD WAS BAD,
BUT IT MADE HIM FURIOUS, MADDER THAN MAD.

I GAVE HIM MY LOYAL LOVE AND DEVOTION,
BUT HE SAID ALL I DID WAS CAUSE TOO MUCH COMMOTION.

HE PUT ME IN THE CAR AND DROVE TO THE PARK.
THEN HE LEFT ME THERE, ALL ALONE IN THE DARK.

I STARTED TO RUN AFTER THE CAR,
BUT I KNEW I'D NEVER MAKE IT—HOME WAS JUST TOO FAR.

I'M A SMART DOG AND WAS INSTANTLY AWARE THAT HE DIDN'T WANT ME. HE JUST DIDN'T CARE.

I WASN'T SURE JUST WHAT TO DO OR WHERE I SHOULD GO.
IF ONLY I COULD FIND ANOTHER HUMAN, I KNOW

THAT SOMEONE WOULD HELP ME OR MAYBE TAKE ME IN.
I'LL HAVE TO BE STRONG AND JUST LIFT UP MY CHIN.

I'LL FIND MY WAY, SOMEHOW, SOMEWHERE.
I KNOW THERE ARE PEOPLE WHO WOULD LOVE ME AND CARE.

I JUST HAVE TO FIND THEM, SO I'LL CONTINUE MY SEARCH.
MAYBE THERE ARE NICE PEOPLE INSIDE THAT CHURCH.

I'LL GO THERE AND WAIT FOR THEM TO COME OUT.
THEN I'LL TELL THEM WHAT HAPPENED, AND I WON'T DOUBT

THAT SOME KIND SOUL WILL TAKE ME HOME, I DON'T
WANT TO BE ALONE JUST LEFT HERE TO ROAM.

SO I SAT NEAR THE CHURCH AND PATIENTLY WAITED.
PEOPLE STARTED COMING OUT—I WAS ELATED!

I WAS JUST SITTING THERE UNDER A TREE WHEN
A MAN AND A LADY WERE APPROACHING ME.

"LOOK AT THAT DOG," I HEARD THEM SAY.
"DOES HE BELONG TO SOMEBODY, OR IS HE A STRAY?"

THE COUPLE CAME OVER, AND THE MAN EXTENDED HIS HAND. THIS WAS HAPPENING JUST AS I'D PLANNED.

I TOLD THEM MY STORY AND THAT I WAS ALONE.
I WAS SCARED AND HUNGRY, THIS I MADE KNOWN.

IN HOPES THAT THEY'D HELP ME AND GIVE ME SOME FOOD,
I DISPLAYED MY CUTENESS AND MY MOST HOPEFUL MOOD.

THE MAN INTRODUCED HIMSELF, SAYING, "MY NAME IS FREDDY, AND THIS IS MY WIFE. HER NAME IS BETTY."

IF YOU WANT TO COME WITH US, GET IN THE CAR.
WE'LL TAKE YOU TO OUR HOUSE—IT ISN'T FAR.

SO I JUMPED RIGHT IN AS FAST AS I COULD.
I HAD A FEELING THIS WOULD TURN OUT TO BE GOOD!

THESE PEOPLE WERE NICE, FRIENDLY, AND KIND.
THEY'RE EXACTLY THE TYPE THAT I HAD IN MIND!

WHEN WE GOT TO THEIR HOUSE, I JUST PLAYED IT COOL.
I TRIED TO BE CALM, NOT BARK OR DROOL.

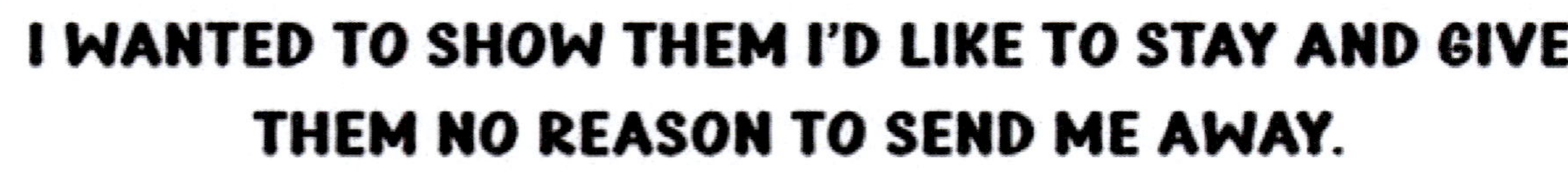
I WANTED TO SHOW THEM I'D LIKE TO STAY AND GIVE THEM NO REASON TO SEND ME AWAY.

THEY SHOWED ME AROUND, AND I LIKED WHAT I SAW.
THIS PLACE WAS PERFECT, AND I WAS IN AWE!

THERE WAS EVEN A BIG, FENCED-IN YARD.
I KNEW LIVING HERE WOULD NOT BE HARD!

I MINDED MY MANNERS AND DISPLAYED GOOD BEHAVIOR.
IF I WANTED TO STAY, THEN I COULD NOT WAVER.

I'D PROVE THAT I COULD BE THE DOG OF THEIR DREAMS.
I'D SHOW THEM I'M WORTHY OF LOVE TO EXTREMES!

THEY CALLED ME TO THE KITCHEN AND PUT DOWN
A PLATE OF THE ODDEST LOOKING FOOD THAT I NEVER ATE.

"TRY IT, YOU'LL LOVE IT," SAID THIS LADY NAMED BETTY.
WE'RE SHARING OUR DINNER. THIS IS SPAGHETTI.

I WALKED TO THE PLATE AND TOOK A WHIFF.
IT SMELLED PRETTY GOOD, SO I CONTINUED TO SNIFF.

"JUST EAT IT," SAID BETTY IN A COMMANDING VOICE.
IF YOU ARE HUNGRY, THEN YOU DON'T HAVE A CHOICE.

SO I TRIED IT, THESE ODD-LOOKING, GOOD-SMELLING STRINGS
AND I DISCOVERED THAT THEY ARE MARVELOUS THINGS!

I GOBBLED IT ALL UP AND WISHED THERE WAS MORE OF THIS FUNNY FOOD CALLED SPAGHETTI THAT I NOW ADORE!

WITH A FULL TUMMY AND A PLACE TO SLEEP,
I HOPED THESE PEOPLE WOULD BE MINE TO KEEP.

THEY MADE ME A BED FROM BLANKETS IN A BOX,
BUT THAT SURE BEAT SLEEPING OUTSIDE ON THE ROCKS.

WE ALL SETTLED IN FOR A QUIET NIGHT.
WHEN MORNING CAME, MUCH TO MY DELIGHT.

FREDDY SAID, "WE'LL TAKE YOU WITH US WHEN WE GO TO WORK.
WE HAVE A JOB FOR YOU, AND IT COMES WITH A PERK!"

"YOU ARE NO LONGER CONSIDERED A STRAY.
YOU ARE OUR TEDDY, AND WE WANT YOU TO STAY!"

"WE OWN A RESTAURANT, AN ITALIAN CAFE.
YOU'LL GO THERE WITH US ALMOST EVERY DAY."

"WE NEED A GREETER, AND YOU ARE IT!
THE WAY WE SEE IT, IT'S A PERFECT FIT."

“WE HELP YOU, AND YOU HELP US. IT’S AS SIMPLE AS THAT—NOTHING MORE TO DISCUSS.”

"YOU'LL GREET ALL THE PEOPLE WHO COME TO EAT. IF THEY LIKE YOU, THEY'LL COME BACK AND MAYBE BRING YOU A TREAT!"

"REMEMBER I TOLD YOU THERE WAS A PERK?
IF YOU DO YOUR JOB WELL AND DO NOT SHIRK

THEN, EVERY DAY, YOU CAN HAVE NOODLES—SPAGHETTI, MACARONI, AND FOR DESSERT, APPLE STRUDELS!"

"SO WHAT DO YOU THINK? WILL YOU DO YOUR BEST?
BETTY AND I BELIEVE YOU CAN PASS THE TEST."

SO I STARTED MY JOB. THERE WERE LOTS OF PEOPLE TO GREET.
I LIKED THEM ALL. THEY WERE NICE TO MEET.

I THINK THEY ALL LIKED ME, TOO,
AND I WAS SO GLAD I HAD THIS JOB TO DO.

JUST AS PROMISED, I GOT LOTS OF NOODLES,
AND I ALSO DISCOVERED I LIKE APPLE STRUDELS!

BUSINESS WAS BOOMING AT THE ITALIAN CAFE, AND TEDDY, THE GREETER, WAS THERE TO STAY!

THE CUSTOMERS KEPT COMING EVERY DAY.
FREDDY AND BETTY LIKE IT THAT WAY!

AND AS FOR TEDDY, HE'S HAPPY TOO THAT
ALL HIS DREAMS HAVE FINALLY COME TRUE!

HE LOVES HIS PEOPLE, AND THEY LOVE HIM.
GONE ARE THE DAYS WHEN LIFE WAS GRIM.

THAT IS THE STORY OF THIS DOG NAMED TEDDY AND HOW HE CAME TO LOVE SPAGHETTI!

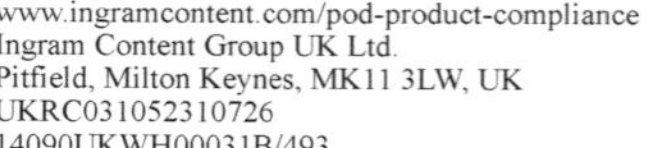

www.ingramcontent.com/pod-product-compliance
Ingram Content Group UK Ltd.
Pitfield, Milton Keynes, MK11 3LW, UK
UKRC031052310726
14090UKWH00031B/493